The Way Children Make Art

The Science Art Method™

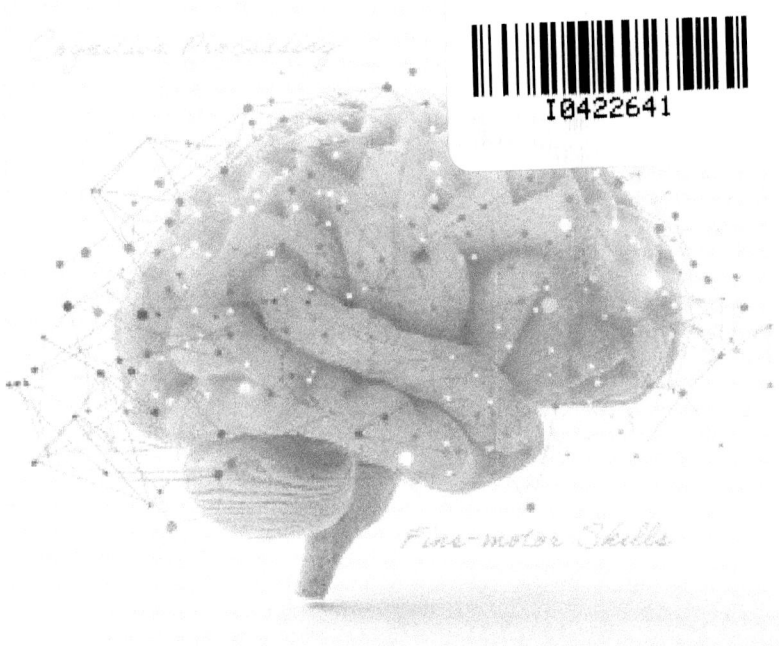

Spramani Elaun

The Way Children Make Art

The Science Art Method

Spramani Elaun

New Edition

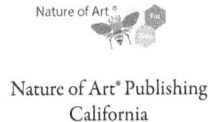

Nature of Art® Publishing
California

♛ Special Invitation ♛

I would like to personally invite you to watch my Art Basic Fundamentals 4 part video series:

- Infant & Toddler – Phases of Art Development
- Ages 3-6 – Phases of Art Development
- Elementary – Phases of Art Development
- Art Basic Fundamentals

This series will help you understand what a child's art program should include. Register by following the link or QR code below.

http://bit.ly/479GxWp

Books By Spramani Elaun

The Way Children Make Art
Defining Visual Arts
Kids Painting
Early Childhood Art Guide
Nurturing Children in the Visual Arts Naturally
Clay Play
Kids Color Theory
Introducing Visual Arts to the Montessori Classroom
Montessori Art – Early Childhood Guide
Montessori Art – The Essential Elementary Guide

Nature of Art® Publishing
P.O. Box 443 Solana Beach, California 92075

First edition published October 30, 2024
Printed in the United States of America
ISBN-979-8991256117

All artwork and photographs were taken in an art classroom or
at special art events hosted By Spramani Elaun.
Contributing Photographers, Mike Hedge

Nature of Art®

Connect With Spramani Online:

EcoKidsArt.com
Montessori-Art.com
Nature-of-art-kids.com
Spramani.com

Facebook.com/nature.of.art
Instagram.com/nature.of.art.kids
Linkedin.com/in/ecokidsart

Dedication

This book is dedicated to my children, Laurun and Spencer.
Lead with your special creative minds.

Contents

Chapter 1

Naturalistic Art Observations

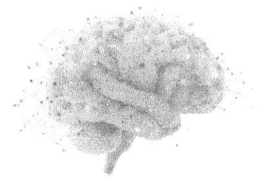

My methodology emerged from a concentrated study of how children develop their artistic visual perception from early childhood through adolescence. Over my years of teaching and making naturalistic observations, I've gained a deep understanding of how art skills develop. I've identified three distinct areas of neurological development that are directly related to the evolution of artistic skill-building over an extended period of time.

My focused observations on children's artistic development began when I started teaching art classes over three decades ago. I made naturalistic observations, studies based on observing subjects in their natural setting in the field. After discovering that traditional fine art instruction does not align with a child's developmental growth, I conceived my method.

Throughout my years of teaching, I observed various types of groups: experimental projects, controlled age group samplings, art class samplings, and public event samplings. I collected journal descriptions and portfolio specimens. I was able to make cross-sectional observations from students who took my classes at different stages of their growth. Additionally, longitudinal observations and samplings came from both my own two children and hundreds of student groups. I have collected art samples from students ranging from toddlers to adolescents.

In my first two decades, I practiced visual arts as a professional; I worked as a graphic designer and art director in the commercial art industry. In my third decade, I opened my own children's art studio, where I taught visual arts to students of various ages.

It was during this time that I began to discern patterns in how children evolve into fine artists. I started documenting my naturalistic observations, and soon I was able to understand how these patterns interconnected and influenced the ways in which children created within all five domains of art.

In my fourth decade, I began applying my unique methodology in a studio-based practice, using this approach exclusively to teach visual arts. As I observed the results, I saw consistent success, which was incredibly encouraging.

I validated this method across a wide range of ages and environments: early childhood, elementary, teens, and adults; in classes, museums, school classrooms, and various pedagogical settings. This method has proven its effectiveness, consistently delivering positive results year after year.

I have developed my own proprietary art teaching system by leveraging the natural structure of a child's sensory processing, known as the phases of art development. I have codified these insights into a preparatory method called SAM (the Science Art Method), which is now my intellectual property. ©2023 All rights reserved. Copyrighted by Spramani Elaun, Nature of Art.

Chapter 2

Discovery of Patterns

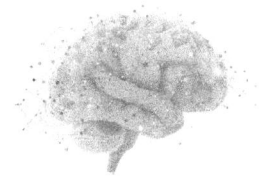

When I first started teaching visual arts, I struggled with teaching children. Although I was a talented and skilled illustrator and painter, teaching kids was challenging at first. One of the main reasons for this struggle was the lack of information available on teaching art to children. There were no books, college courses, or online programs on how to develop art programming for youngsters.

Plenty of resources focused on teaching adults and teens but not the primary grades or early childhood. Everything was geared towards how more mature students learn fine art.

My initial approach was to teach children like little artists, using the same ideas I had learned in college but with simpler lessons. However, I found it difficult to get my students to see and plan like artists. I was teaching them complex topics like the Elements and Principles of Design and asking them to look at still-life subjects to draw and paint. Within the first few years, I learned that such tasks were too challenging for young children. It was the traditional way adult artists learned, but it wasn't suitable for them.

During those early years, I observed my son casually drawing on his own at age five after attending a guided drawing session with other children his age. He had perfectly followed directions and drawn an apple tree along with the other students. However, when he drew on his own, he doodled and couldn't create anything realistic, even though he copied well in my classroom.

His doodles were silly, abstract, and not representational like his classroom work. I found it strange that children could follow directions and copy but couldn't use those skills to create their own ideas independently.

At that stage, I realized the lessons I was teaching

were not helping and were far too advanced. I started to think children needed more foundational lessons before progressing to advanced concepts. As a homeschool parent, I attracted many homeschool families to my art classes. Unlike traditional school or after-school art programs, I had multiple age groups in my classes simultaneously. Most homeschool students attended my classes with all their siblings, ranging from toddlers to teens. Sometimes, even the parents participated in making art. This unique setting allowed me to observe multiple ages doing exactly the same art lesson and to identify interesting patterns across the different age groups.

I noticed that younger students struggled to understand and see what I saw when I directed them to look at something, whereas older children could identify objects or images and grasp the ideas I explained. One thing I observed was each child's visual perception. Children found it difficult to draw something they had no prior knowledge of or thoughts about.

For example, a young boy struggled with my guided lessons but became excited and successful in drawing a dump truck filled with tomatoes after a weekend trip with his family. His excitement and personal experience of seeing this empowered him to follow my directions and create an original drawing. Through these observations, I learned that three neural activities—visual perception, cognitive processing, and fine-motor capabilities— were crucial to children's ability to create art.

After recognizing this, I set aside all the ideas I learned in college and focused on nurturing these three sensory processing systems through my art lessons. My art programming developed around the phases of art development in these sensory areas for each age group.

I also discovered that too much copy-mode work stifles creativity and that children ages eight to twelve struggle with drawing realistic images due to a lack of fine-motor practice. This often leads them to believe they are not artistic. Many foundational drawing skills are commonly overlooked before tackling complex steps in traditional art teaching models.

After years of using this teaching methodology, I became a skilled art teacher, capable of teaching almost every child at any age. While I couldn't teach toddlers to paint and draw detailed images,

I could create lessons that built their foundational knowledge through process-based activities, preparing them for the next building block of art knowledge. I could effectively teach children in the elementary grades drawing, painting, and color theory, leading to realistic imagery.

By focusing on the three sensory art patterns, I could quickly assess visual art knowledge and adapt art lessons. This became my method of teaching called the Science Art Method™ (SAM), which uses the three sensory systems to teach art, develop art lessons, and create curriculum.

Science Art Method™

This method is based on how children develop artistically through their senses and acquire fine art skills. The science art method uses the structure of the brain, working with the child's natural multisensory system and growth rate. It supports artistic development by acknowledging hierarchical neural connections as the children process art lessons in stages. As they grow, children are wiring neural networks of information. The Science Art Method framework encompasses the three crucial parts of the child's developing sensory system:

Different growth phases of art development: digital doodle from early childhood through adolescence

Visual perception – the visual cortex system

Cognitive processing – the memory and neural network system

Fine motor skills – the sensorimotor movement control system

Within these three areas of neural activity lie secondary skills that I will discuss in Chapters 6-9:

- Tactile learning and fine motor skills
- Implicit memory
- Spatial intelligence
- Dynamic and static spatial understanding

Finally, I conclude the book with a discussion of how art education can foster children's development in all of these crucial areas.

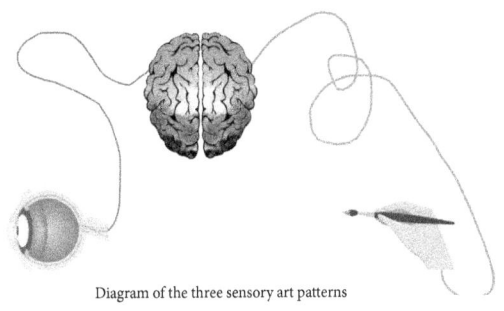

Diagram of the three sensory art patterns

Chapter 3

Connecting Visual Growth

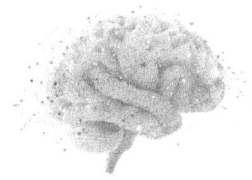

Visual perception is one of the key aspects of how children develop artistic skills. This is the most exciting part of my Science Art Method and why I nurture visual arts slowly through adolescence. I've discovered that a child's visual history affects creativity, imagination, and their level of artistic skills at different stages of growth.

Each individual child will learn, think, and store experiences as they gather visual information in their own personal world. Visual perception is directly linked to how a child expresses visual ideas, draws, paints, and learns to construct artworks. Artworks uniquely express each person's own visual perceptions. Visual perception is the key to understanding how children develop into artists.

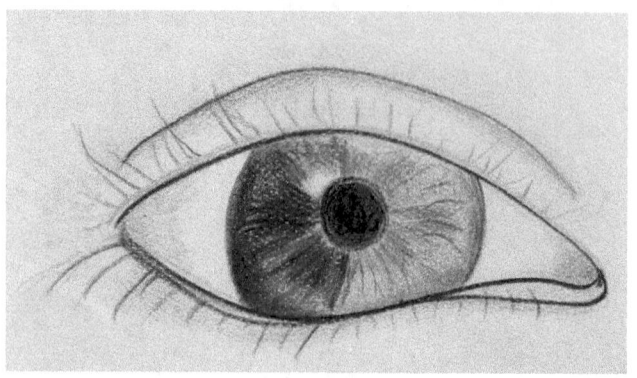
Illustration by Spramani Elaun

What Does Visual Perception Mean?

Visual perception comes when many things happen in concert. You collect light information with your retinal ganglion cells, and then messages travel to the brain to activate neural networks of visual representations of images and memories for object recognition. By collecting data from our field of vision and processing our thoughts, our visual perception occurs.

We might say that visual perception is an afterthought following something we have looked at: Gathering + Thinking = Visual Perception. Visual perception can also mean visual intellect. This is a generalized explanation of how our neural networks function. For young children, it is a bottom-up cognitive process.

Humans Don't See with Eyes Only!

What I'm about to say may seem unintuitive because most of us think our eyes see objects exactly as we think of them in the physical environment. The fact is, our eyes don't see objects or images at all. Our eyes don't see anything; they are simply the doorway to absorb light! Our eyes absorb light, then transmit neural signals, and then the magic of understanding what we are seeing happens inside our brain. Our brain helps us actually understand an optical projection in our visual field. Our eyes gather the light information and transmit signals through neural pathways from the eyes to the primary visual cortex. This activates our visual history, which then forms our visual perception on what is in front of us.

The Eyes' Role in Gathering Information

The human eye is the most important sense organ we have. We send vital information to our brain by using our visual system. Our visual system includes field of vision and retinal ganglion cell networks. The first stage of visual sensation starts with the interface between an optical projection and our retinas. Retinas sense light through our photoreceptive rods and cones, which then transfer this information into our complex nerve networks. Our visual neural system then sends signals to different places in the brain, retrieving data from our memory system for object recognition. From our limited knowledge in the field of neuroscience to present day, this is how object recognition happens.

Our Retinas

Our retinas sense light, and then the visual processing starts by transferring information into complex nerve networks for understanding. Here is what is known: Our eyes detect incoming light, and the retina transduces it into neural signals. That information flows to our visual system, like the values of light, motion, direction, line edges, orientation of edges, form, color, pattern, spatial information, and other higher order visual processing still undiscovered by neuroscience. The different patterns of light captured in our visual field provide the information we need for our nervous system to understand what's physically in our view. The main role of our eyes is to gather electromagnetic light information.

Our visual field can detect 180 degrees horizontally and 130 degrees vertically (see Visual field diagram on page 27). This field is referred to as our cone of vision. Another fascinating thing to note is this light information travels in thousandths of seconds to a midline and then to the visual cortex of the opposite hemisphere. (Ackerman © Discovering the Brain 1992.)

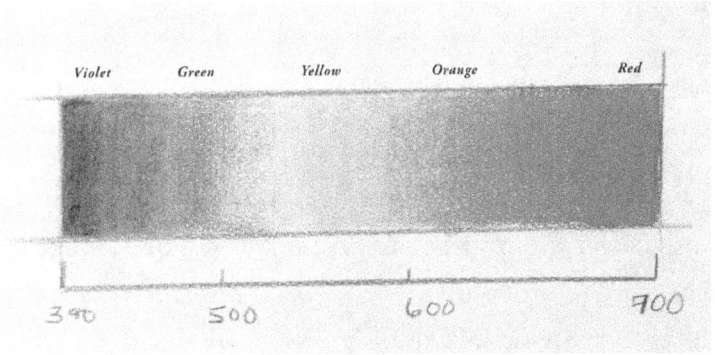

Illustration of the electromagnetic visual spectrum ranging from 390 to 700 nanometers

Color

The retina contains three types of receptor cone cells, which give us humans color vision. Our color vision is also known as trichromatic color vision, with cones that can sense red, green, and blue. Human retinas can detect only the electromagnetic visual spectrum ranging from 390 to 700 nanometers. Color vision happens when

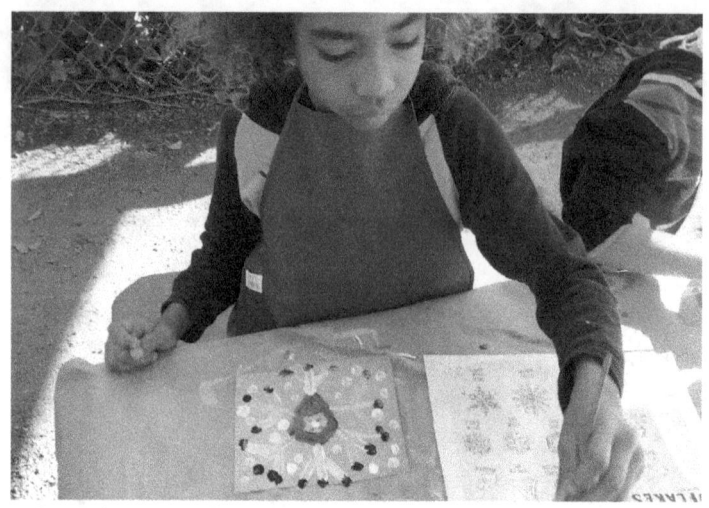

Student acrylic painting: different color values of blue

we receive light information through our cone receptors. Light can be affected by atmosphere, moisture, and night or day light sources or damaged rod and cone photoreceptors. These effects can alter wavelengths when viewing objects. We do not always experience exactly the same visuals from one person to another, which causes us to perceive things, including color, individually and sometimes differently.

Creating What Is Known

When a child looks at an optical projection, they will not be able to draw a photographic copy of the exact image. They will only be able to draw what they have understood and experienced by

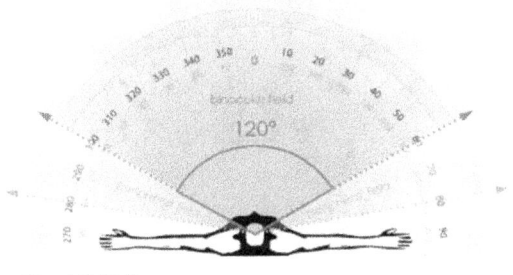
Visual field diagram

their own visual perception or intellect at that time in their development. What an adult sees versus what a young child sees depends on their visual experiences and history.

Gaining artistic knowledge takes years! It is essential to understand the laws of nature's perspectives, environmental surroundings, fine motor movements, self-equilibrium, self-awareness of gravitational existence in temporal space, sensory tactile experience through touching 3D forms and different sizes, and liquid and solid objects.

So even if you want a child to copy an image exactly, their visual perception needs to be developed somewhat in terms of the optical projection. You can't judge a child's drawing abilities through copy-mode work because you both see completely differently. A child must understand an optical projection to make marks that resemble it, plus have the motor control to make shapes and forms.

19

During these early phases of art development, children should work in a balance of creative-mode and copy-mode art making, which I will discuss further in the next section. Again, children in the formative years will not be drawing from top-down brain processing but rather from bottom-up brain processing.

Copy Mode vs. Creative Mode

I've created these two terms to explain two models of instruction. They both have their value in art programming. I'm discussing them here so you can understand the terms as I use them broadly in this book. I discuss these two teaching modes at greater length in my teaching guides.

Copy Mode

Copy mode refers to systematic, step-by-step art instruction. The general premise is that a student learns to draw by mimicking or copying a visual image step by step. This method is sometimes used to teach drawing or painting skills. Students learn to draw by studying perspective rendering, shade, light, value, line, forms, and composition, copying what they see in their field of vision.

Fine illustrators make realistic artwork by being mature in all the component skills to make accurate copy-mode drawings. Copy-mode drawing can help develop muscles in students' eyes, hands, and memories. Copying geometric or organic shapes can help students achieve similar shapes they might desire in their own creative drawings or designs.

Making copy-mode artwork, however, is not possible for a young child. Limit the copy-mode and step-by-step drawing lessons you offer to children in early childhood and lower elementary grades.

Creative Mode

Making art in creative mode gives children free range to conjure up their own ideas, which supports the artistic process standards. When children learn to create from their own ideas, they conceptualize original artworks through thought, imagination, spatial awareness, planning, and constructing.

These are the qualities of a creative innovator. Because young children have great imaginations,

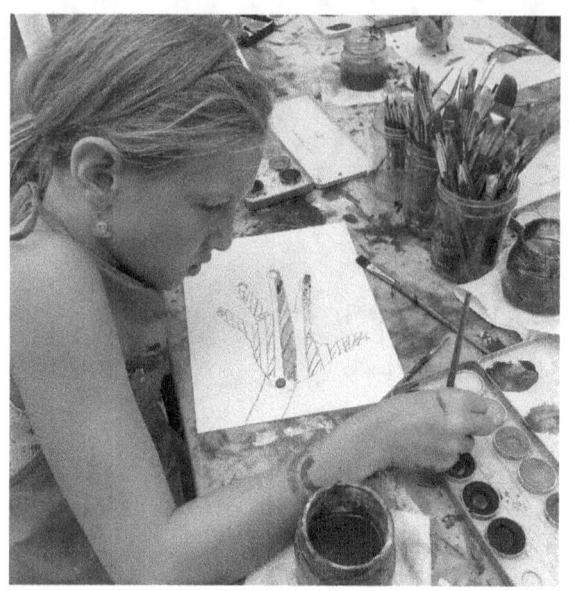
Art camp student creating unique line elements inside her hand print.

it's ideal for them to being making art this way. You can show children examples of projects using similar mediums and techniques but give them the freedom to come up with their own ideas of images, colors, and even different techniques for finishing their artworks.

Young children should start with making art in a creative mode, then bridge to simple line, shape, and/or form copy-mode lessons. Creative mode is how I start to nurture child-led art projects. I introduce an art project, demonstrate the medium, and usually give no point of reference—an image, for example—for them to copy; I simply allow kids to work in a process-based way.

Usually, they simply explore the medium and conjure up their own creative images from their imaginations and experiments. Creative imagination consists of original thoughts and ideas that emerge from one's own personal reflections and visual history. This is the opposite of copy-mode drawings, which are not original.

Symbolic Imagery Is Not Readiness for Drawing Lessons

Writing and holding a pencil is not readiness for children's drawing lessons. There are many reasons why adults or teachers might think otherwise. First, young children are capable of duplicating the twenty-six letters of the alphabet and ten numbers. Writing comes naturally for a child, because letters are solid, light, line-edge information for visual pathways to sense. Letters and numbers are similar because they use simple straight and curved lines.

Learning the alphabet uses other sensory inputs like touch, vision, and the auditory system. When all sensory systems are firing together, children learn difficult concepts more easily.

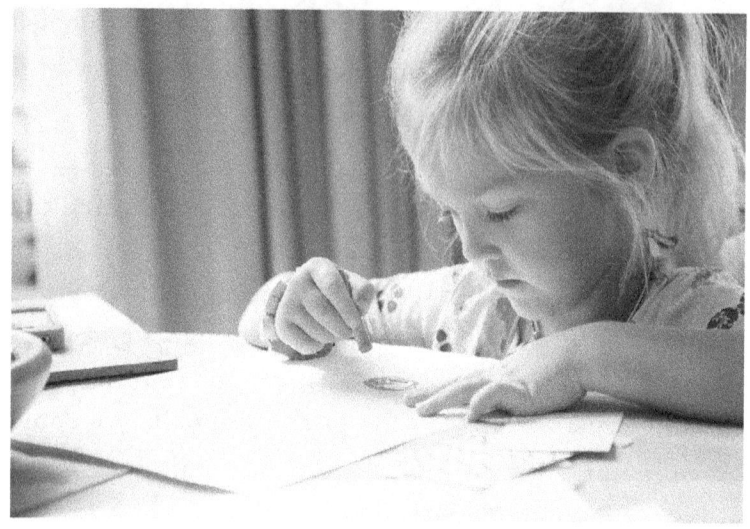

Student drawing lines and shapes with oil pastels.

Early childhood students making line and shape brushmarks with watercolor."

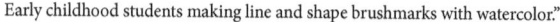

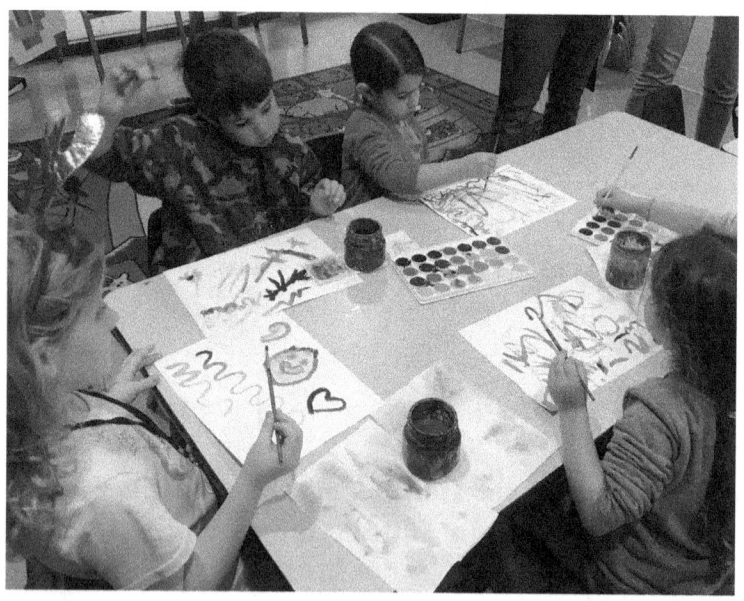

In a short time, they can achieve dexterity with a pencil. Simple shapes like circles, ovals, and straight lines can then be learned quickly. Learning to write can come easily for young children, but again, it doesn't prepare them for advanced realistic drawing concepts.

Symbolic Line-Edge Forms First

A child's first marks are in line form, and there are many reasons for this. First, from what we currently understand, our early visual system develops topographical hierarchy maps, starting with objects recognized by our edge-enhancing cells. These cells assemble maps starting by recognizing oriented edges, then moving to other complex segmentation systems for recognition. Because of this, I recommend that children start with learning different lines, then move to drawing lines into shapes. Simple line forms are easier to see and comprehend because there's no difficult rendering details, just edges.

Generally, most children draw symbolic line drawings during the period from four to ten years old. It's very healthy for a child to be doodling and drawing in lines first. Many cognitive processing activities and visual perception experiences must occur before children can make their symbolic line forms turn into realistic three-dimensional drawings.

I recommend introducing drawing lessons by starting with simple lines, line shapes, line textures, patterns, coloring in simple line shapes, then moving into color values. After lots of practice with these types of lessons, you can move into realism in the upper elementary grades. Then transition into light and shadow, three-dimensional form lessons, and linear perspective drawing concepts.

So, start with basic symbolic line shapes that children know well, both geometric and organic. Geometric shapes include squares, circles, triangles etc. Then introduce simple objects with similar shapes, like a ball, leaf, dog, stick figures of their family—things they are familiar with in their environment. Start with flat two-dimensional objects with clear line edges, then transition slowly into three-dimensional beginner renderings. When children reach adolescence, you can then train their eyes to see natural perspective and all the techniques to make their artworks look realistic.

Visual Perception Is Purposeful and Selective

It's important to note that visual perception is purposeful and selective when we have an optical projection in our eyes' focus and in our mind's focus as well. Many things can be in our visual field but out of focus because we are not cognitively processing a particular object in that visual field. Not having focus or point of interest keeps us from seeing things or understanding what we are looking at.

Have you ever looked in a certain direction and not noticed something until you really focused in on it? You need both actions to occur, visual and cognitive focus. Our sight can be looking into a visual field but not see until we focus and try to understand what we are actually viewing. Many times, I have walked into a room and not noticed anything until I was looking for something in particular, and suddenly, details of objects became clear and focused.

I make a special note here to explain why purposeful and selective meaning is important and related to this art method. Child-led art projects are purposeful and selective. When children create artwork of their own interest, I have had higher success teaching difficult concepts in painting and drawing lessons.

Here's an example of how purposeful and

selective visual perception plays its role in teaching artistic skills and helps children create child-led art: A young student of mine wanted to try watercolor painting but found it very difficult and declared it was impossible to learn. Frustrated, he explained how he had no talent for this medium.

I suggested he paint things he was interested in and loved. The student announced he loved dragons and knew everything about these mystical creatures. As I set out painting supplies, he spouted a litany of facts to me about dragons. This student spent a couple hours in my art space and painted numerous versions of dragons with watercolor—without feeling frustrated.

He happily talked about dragon lore and painted many different versions of the creatures as he experimented and explored watercolor. He was open to learning different techniques and visited me in my art studio a few times more. He also felt comfortable experimenting with other mediums during those visits.

Having identified that visual perception is purposeful and selective, I used this to my advantage to teach this student beginning watercolor skills, working harmoniously with the innate child-led interest and range of semi-motor abilities.

Visual Perception for Survival

Our eyes and brain evolved for us to survive our environment, not to study visual arts. We start developing visual perception from the day we are born, and it never ends till our life cycle is over. Our visual system has been evolving from the beginning of mankind's known existence. We have great evidence from pictorial records and treasures uncovered by archaeologists from the past to present day. Hunting and gathering were typical images confirming our existence, striving to survive as a culture. The use of human consciousness in making art and tools is estimated to date back to 60,000 years ago.

The evolution of how we became visual communicators is not new. Recent scientific communities, such as the neural, cognitive, and optical sciences, give new answers to understanding how visual perception relates to our evolving consciousness. Our visual system is certainly not new, but activities such as appreciating static artworks are relatively a modern activity—less than a few hundred years old—especially compulsory art teaching in primary and secondary schools. Our complex optical system was not developed to

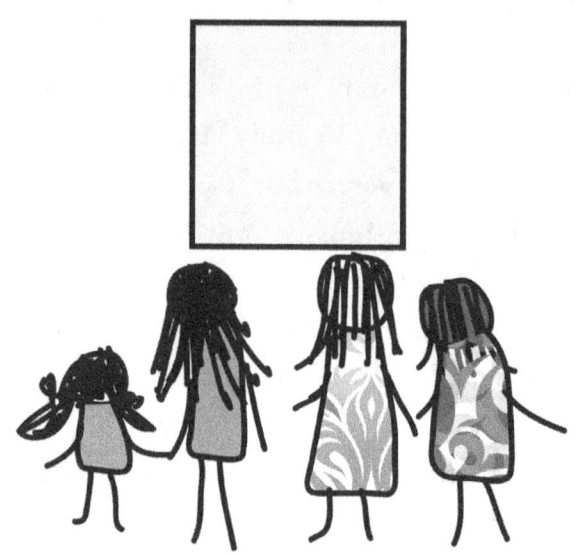

Four generations viewing the same art: digital doodle by my daughter, myself, mother, and grandmother.

stare at visual artwork nor concentrate and make sense of it.

Studying arts through our visual sensory system is a fairly new activity for man. We have evolved over the last 600 years to communicate and conceptualize our visual perceptions as a new way of expressing ourselves through art creation. Today we live in a highly visual world, and this could be why our society is gravitating toward understanding visual arts more; it may be one of our new survival skills in future times.

Visual Perception Is Individual

I would like to present this final example to help you comprehend the importance of the role that visual perception plays when young children are learning to draw, paint, or sculpt. Picture four generations of your family walking into a museum together. I picture my grandmother, my mother, myself, and my young daughter at age six. All four of us walk up to a painting and focus on the optical images. All four of us get into the visual pathway of this painting and view the same painting...or do we?

We all collect similar light data from our field of vision, which is transmitted via neurons to our brain. Remember all the information we collect with our retinas—like light, visible lines, edges, colors, forms, and shape.

If we are looking at a painting from the turn of the nineteenth century featuring objects of that particular era, each of us will cognitively process different thoughts. We will conjure up different types of information, individually retrieving our autobiographical memories of the objects or experiences.

My grandmother may have used something similar in her lifetime and have vivid memories to recall; she will notice all the details of the objects painted. She will be using top-down processing. My mother may have seen these things around when she was younger or be able to recall vague memories of them. I might have read stories about these objects in history books or seen them in old movies but have never seen them up close, in real life. With no spatial awareness stored in my mind, I might be visualizing how these objects were operated.

My daughter may be looking at something completely foreign and be unable to make sense of the objects or even focus on them, because there is nothing like them in her day-to-day experience. She will have no experiential history stored in her mind. My daughter will be scanning by bottom-up processing triggered by the retinal stimulus.

Each of us will gather visual sensory information to process what we see in our minds. All four of us will create our own judgments and inferences and come up with our own visual perception of the painting.

Here I must make the statement, "Children draw what they see and know best." It should now be clear that teaching a child to copy or study the Old Masters' artwork is not aligned with their growth phases. No person redraws images without visual perception taking place or recalling autobiographical memories.

I recognized that children could artistically draw best when they had plenty of knowledge and firsthand experience with what they were trying to copy or creatively imagine. When a child actually touched an object, saw it in action, or understood its function, they had better success recreating it in their artworks. They were more interested in learning the art lesson at hand.

Respect a child's individual visual perception. What you understand and think is beautiful and meaningful to paint or draw may be much different than what interests your student.

Chapter 4

Cognitive Mind/Brain Processing

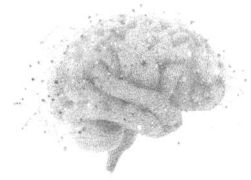

Children grow two ways: physically by growing their body and cognitively by developing their mind/brain. Brain and body maturation is so accelerated that within a few years, a child can become unrecognizable to family and friends who see them infrequently. This rapid growth to adulthood seems almost like magic. Humans grow well into their mid-twenties in physical attributes.

Indeed, knowledge can be gained throughout a person's life span. This growth through early childhood and adolescence affects how children experience and learn visual arts in comparison to adults.

Cognitive Brain Growth

We can't see the brain growing or gaining knowledge, but it's happening! The brain also grows at an enormous speed, like the body. If you examine the size of an infant's head in relation to their body size, you can see tremendous growth from childhood to adolescence. Brain maturation goes beyond physical body growth; cognitive growth is always improving but is less visible.

Cognition goes on inside our brain. It explains the thought process in our minds. Cognitive and neural changes happen as we develop. Cognitive thoughts lead to gained knowledge, memories, comprehension, problem-solving ability, conceptualization, creativity, new information processing, self-regulation through executive function, and personal inferences.

Neural input and output stimuli are happening during art creation. Our sensory system inputs stimulate cognitive processing. Sensory processing is transmitted, processed, and stored within our declarative or non-declarative memory. When it's happening, networks of nerve cells are connecting. Billions of neurons are wiring together and making connections. This is a generalized explanation of cognition.

Here's the best way I can describe what cognition

would look like while a child creates art: During art experiences, a child collects input stimuli from their senses—their eyes, hands, and ears. Sensory inputs travel via neural networks that communicate to many different brain regions, like the primary visual cortex, primary motor cortex, and somatosensory cortex, resulting in our retrieval of experiential history, stored schema, memories, personal inferences, memory recall, and associations of past art projects.

Then the child's visual perception is formed, and the result is new neural networks firing off signals, then finally, the child responds by sensorimotor movement, exploring or creating by physically making movements with their hands. Gaining new knowledge, expressing emotions, and exploring concepts and mediums are all possible when a child creates art. This can all be described as cognitive development.

Building Cognitive Network Blocks of Knowledge

The functioning of cognition is an essential part of how children learn art or understand the laws of nature's perspective. No art would exist without brain cognition. It's important that teachers understand that neural networks are

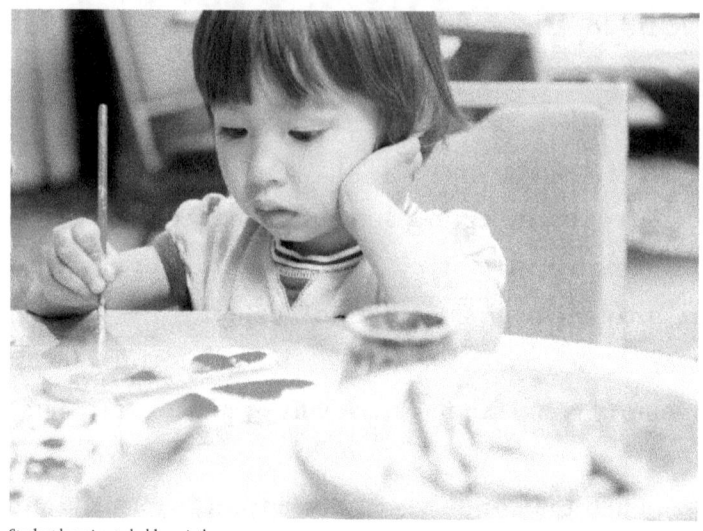
Student learning to hold a paintbrus.

always expanding and building knowledge in these critical years.

Children don't learn art in the same way as adults because their brains are still growing. They are learning art for the first time with no art experience in their memory, no neural networks developed, and no advanced visual perception yet.

Despite what we know now in the twenty-first century, how art relates to the brain and the mind's eye is still very unclear. More needs to be learned about the psychological aspect of visual perception related to the visual arts.

Our brain is part of our central nervous system enclosed within the skull; it contains billions of neurons. Neuroscientists have made astonishing discoveries about the nature of the brain's functions. However, this research is slow, and even now, we are just scratching the surface of understanding why and how our brain works.

My observations on how children come into their own visual perception goes against what we commonly believe about how children make art. My advice is to nurture cognitive art processing and be flexible through their young phases of art development.

In the early childhood years, I recommend that children build blocks of visual art knowledge, wiring neural networks of information by bottom-up processing. Bottom-up processing is sensory, data-driven information collected by the brain in real time with no prior knowledge. Also, give children time to develop executive function by conjuring up their own mental thought processes.

This learning should develop slowly in early childhood. Children should learn in layers in order to build a strong foundation of understanding. These sequential layers should come by positive repetitive art experiences, art problem-solving, and lots of exploring.

It is also important to follow the four steps of the artistic process as established by the national core art standards: investigation, imagination, construction, and reflection. Providing many positive sequences of making art can build blocks of deep knowledge.

Be sure to apply no pressure to produce satisfying artwork for an audience. A child's confidence and self-esteem can stay intact without pressure to please or produce artwork for an audience. Art skills will progress naturally by building blocks of knowledge as they grow into their adolescent years.

Chapter 5

Sensory Art Learning

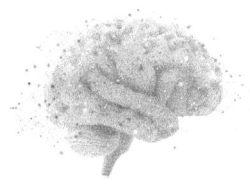

Visual sensory processing, cognition, and fine motor processing are all linked together. Our senses include vision, touch, scent, hearing, and taste. This system plays a vital role in how we gather information from the environment around us.

Collected sensory information is transmitted electronically to our brain networks. Our different neural networks are always communicating; this can also be explained as cognitive processing, which is beneficial for deep learning and comprehension.

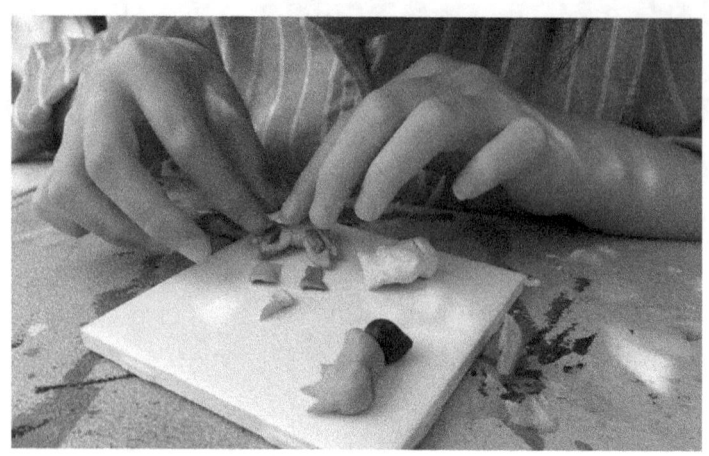

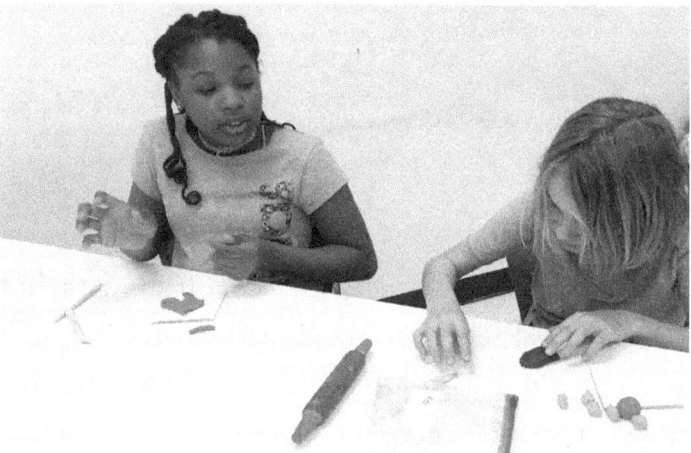

Elementary students learning how to clay model.

Tactile Learning by Sensory Touch

Tactile learning can be described as feeling by touching with one's own hands. When a child touches an object, sensory messages are transmitted to the somatosensory cortex. Tactile sensations can help children learn and understand by touch.

Visual art learning can also happen from direct touching with the hands. Tactile art making stimulates learning in different ways than visual or audio learning. For a developing child, tactile exploration can also lead to better fine motor function and control.

Tactile learning is recommended for highly active children or those with kinesthetic learning styles. Many children learn better by physical movement and tactile sensory stimulus. Children with visual, hearing, and linguistical impairments benefit greatly from tactile activities.

A child's manipulations or produced artwork reveal their understanding based upon combined visual and tactile sensory processing experiences. It's becoming increasingly important for young children to have sensory tactile exploration opportunities in

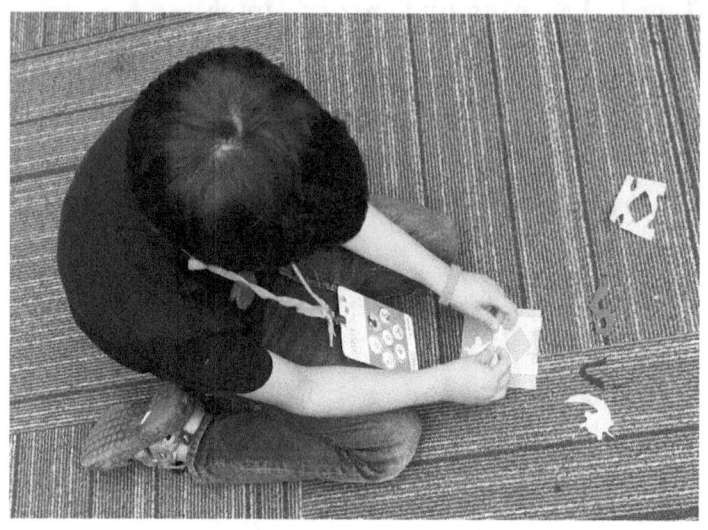
Elementary student designing geometric patterns with sticker styrofoam.

their younger years. Visual arts experiences are a perfect way to experience tactile sensation.

Almost all art making requires using direct touch to construct and build or to express with a medium. Without tactile opportunities, a child can miss out on important temporal and spatial learning. Learning and creating through touch helps build brain connectivity that can't come from just sight and hearing alone.

Tactile art exploration is crucial for children. I recommend providing lots of sensory art experiences. Try out many different art projects involving hand manipulations that can aid in learning. Provide blocks of time for students to engage their hands and fingers directly.

Tactile Art Making Is Beneficial for Stress Relief

Over my years of naturalistic art observations, I've witnessed tactile art projects leading children into relaxed states of mind time and time again. I've seen them come into my classroom highly stressed and then quickly transition into calm relaxation as they focus on their handiwork.

Most art activities engage multiple senses and can help children relax and work calmly. Tactile art making stimulates processing in response to the child's sense of touch. This processing takes place in the left and right hemispheres of the brain simultaneously, helping children enter an active multisensory learning state.

Strong connectivity occurs, and the child becomes intensely focused on his or her activity. Children using their hands can be so engaged that other stress-related thoughts clear their minds, and they enter flow states. They can forget the stress they were experiencing before entering the creative flow state.

All the processing from different senses has a calming effect. Tactile sensations allow children to focus solely on their creative process while they form or manipulate with their hands. It's good for children during their early years to develop good habits and activities that can help regulate their own relaxation by engaging in creative handiwork.

I've coined the phrase active multisensory learning to explain this cognitive state I've witnessed time after time. Children can transition from a stressful, chaotic emotional state to an active multisensory learning state and become relaxed by their hand manipulations. Tactile art making can relieve stress for kids!

When children reach the ages of three to six, it's possible to start teaching them visual art skills. This can be considered building multisensory integration, learning in the three key component areas, and initiating cross-sensory experiences.

With directed sensory input and experiences, children learn to see and record memories of the art elements, verbalize art element terms, and work tacitly to develop fine motor movement. Learning to make brushstrokes or drawing different lines or form and manipulate tools in clay modeling all boost multisensory development. Neurons respond to cross-modal stimulation in combination with external art sensory experiences.

Teaching the brain sequential temporal and spatial art information can wire neurons together. In my naturalistic observations, I've witnessed students at these early ages learning foundational art skill sets, then advancing to more complex and controlled motor development.

Chapter 6

Fine Motor Movement

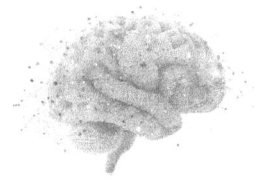

S ensorimotor development is a physical attribute that advances as children grow. Fine motor control helps with creating art projects and using art materials. When fine motor control is achieved, a child can make marks with a paintbrush; doodle, draw, and sketch with a pencil; and sculpt or build with their own hands.

These movements become possible with full control of muscles. Developing fine-tuned motor control takes years for young children, unlike adults. Children gain motor development skills as they learn to control small muscles.

These can be in their fingers, hands, arms, and even around the eyes. Once a child achieves control of these small muscles, it becomes easier to learn art skills and explore techniques.

Sensorimotor movement provides vital information for the developing nervous system. Movement is connected to our sensory systems' wiring for tactile, audio, visual, and balance. The brain receives stimulating feedback from motion. This feedback stimulates more sensory inputs, as opposed to just looking at something. When movement is involved, neural networks are better stimulated. The experience of the movement is constant neural looping feedback, helping cognition.

Very young children start with gross movement, then develop more refined motor control. This fine motor control helps with complex hand dexterity. Integrating multisensory stimuli helps make adjustments in motor control over time. These movements become possible with full control of muscles. Gross to fine motor development has been linked to stimulating higher cognitive processes.

Gaining mastery with movements can help children with paintbrush strokes, mixing and achieving colors, grasping, applying and adjusting pressure, holding a pencil, making marks or doodling, squeezing, pressing, pushing, manipulating clay into a form, and tearing and cutting hand movements.

Fine Motor Skills Are Linked to Art Making

Understand that to become artistically skillful, fine motor control has to happen first. Try to provide lots of repetitive art movements in the younger years to help children go from gross to fine motor control as they develop.

Remember, children at the same ages can be at different intellectual and physical phases of development, so I recommend lots of repetition. All instruction sequences can be the same, but they will never affect every child in the same way. Each child cognitively processes information differently depending on their developmental stage in life, art experience, knowledge, and interests.

Provide multiple art lessons to practice using large and small muscles. Many art projects can look different but have the same skill-building benefits for artistic fine motor control.

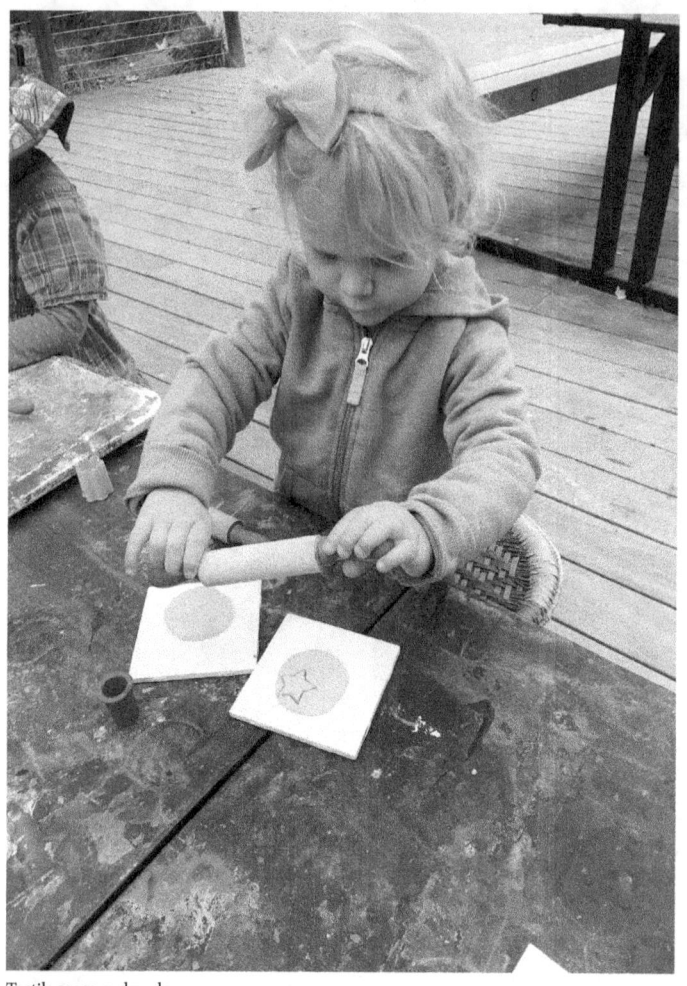
Tactile sensory clay play.

For example, in the younger years, let children play with large paintbrushes for larger brushstrokes, then move to smaller paintbrushes for smaller, more controlled strokes, either with many different projects or the same style of project.

For example, start with movements controlled by the full arm, then move to elbow movements, and finally refined wrist paintbrush or pencil movements. When I approach early childhood children painting, they start out gross with uncontrolled full-arm movements.

By ages four to six years, children start using their elbows to hands, and finally in upper grades, they are able to move their wrists and fingers to fully control their drawing or painting marks.

Early Art-Making Movements Can Build Brain Intelligence

You may think visual art activities are just filling in gaps of time, merely busywork for children.

But the action of making art is doing a lot of positive things for kids simply by implementing these types of movements. Most art creation requires hand dexterity and sensorimotor learning to develop muscle memory in the hand and fingers. Educators can play a vital role in how they design their movement activities and what they offer their students in the classroom.

In recent years, researchers have established that early motor movement develops better cognitive academic performance in the later grades. Practicing motor movement early, even starting in infancy, can directly affect cognitive development and children's readiness for learning.

A child's genetic profile as well as their experiences can predict good cognitive performance. Studies done in the United Kingdom have found correlations between typical motor milestones and their direct effect on cognitive development when the children begin primary school.

Lack of opportunities to develop gross to fine motor skills leaves young student at risk in their physical readiness to be physically independent when reaching primary grades. Aside from other important aspects of development, such as nutrition, emotional stability, and social support, building gross to fine motor skill has been linked to stimulating higher cognitive processes.

Typical activities like clay modeling, painting, coloring, gluing, pasting, cutting, selecting, and arranging helps develop gross to refined movement. This ability helps with complex hand dexterity, integration of multisensory stimuli, and making adjustments in motor control.

Early childhood students can benefit tremendously by starting art programs early. Over years, the students increase the virtuosity of their movements. Most importantly, early art education builds the necessary technical skills needed to advance in other domains.

Chapter 7

Implicit Memory

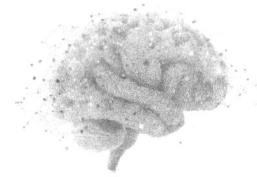

Implicit memory develops neural nets that connect automatically without being the person being conscious of it or thinking about the task at hand. When children practice repeated movements, they're reenforcing nondeclarative, implicit memory—the actions are wired and become linked in their brain.

That means they don't have to consciously think about every minute action; they will see a paintbrush and instinctively know to pick it up, dip it into the palette or water, and start painting.

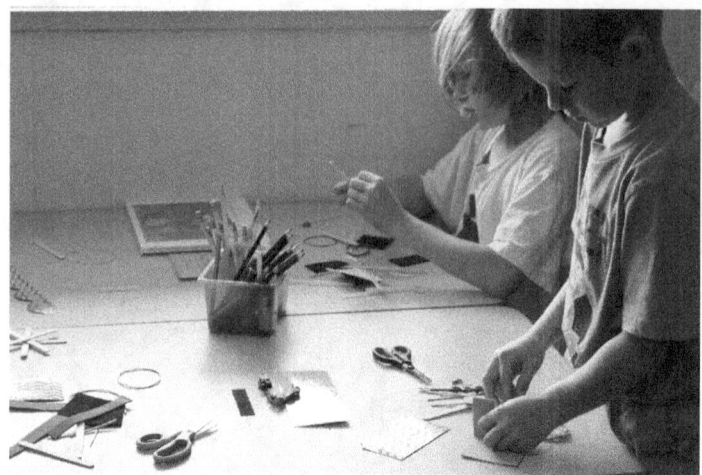

Elementary students constructing crafts.

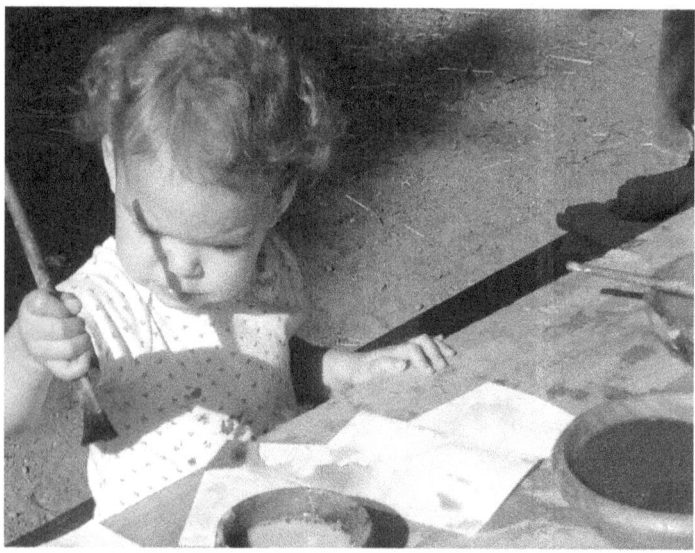

Early childhood student learning how to dip a paintbrush into paint.

The next time they engage in an art activity, implicit memory kicks in, and their hand movements will come more naturally. Holding a paintbrush immediately sends that information to their brain, triggering an implicit memory action. This is known to develop the prefrontal cortex and associated areas. Implicit memory plays a huge role in building top-down, hierarchical art skills for children to recall.

The foundation of the Science Art Method™ builds the child's implicit memory through hands-on motor practice. The students experience the temporal order of actions in multistep sequences. They can work on a number of artistic movements, then move to more systematic complex motor movements as their art skills develop. Students will come to have automatic movements that don't require conscious thought.

By building implicit memory, children can enter the primary grades and quickly advance into learning new artistic techniques and developing muscle memory. This will be possible because they retrieve implicit memory from earlier learned tasks in a top-down processing fashion.

Some of these early tasks may be loading a paintbrush, managing art materials with ease, and fine motor brushstroke application. This prepares the child to learn the next challenging skill sets, like blending paint—mixing tints, shades, and values without having to struggle to learn new semi-motor movements at the same time.

Building implicit memory helps them develop more skills down the road; they'll have this memory stored in their brain and can then focus on new skills.

Chapter 8

Spatial Intelligence

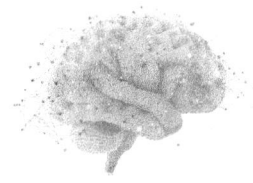

Visual spatial intelligence is a learned mental process of understanding relations between objects. Spatial learning is recorded in our memory. We develop it by creating with elements in space. This is understanding of perspective—space between elements in two dimensions, geographical placement, and the position of arranged items in three-dimensional space.

Spatial learning is formed through multisensory gathering of dynamic motion or by viewing static imagery results. Over time, this builds spatial intelligence. Sight patterns help with mapping

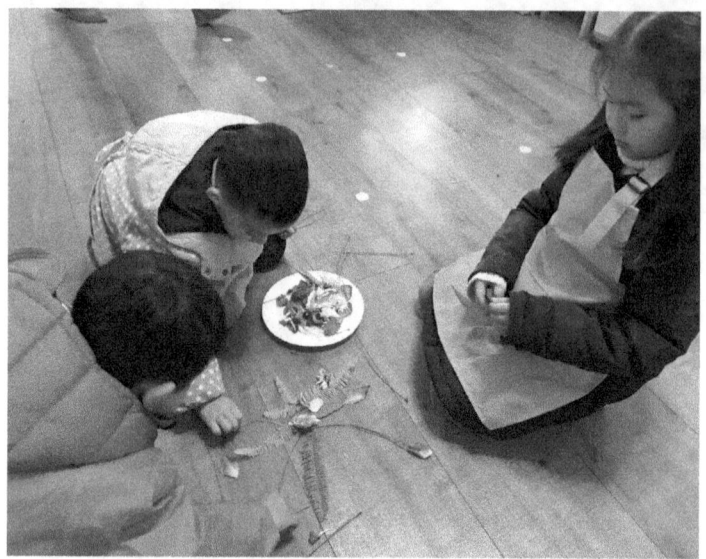
Arranging natural mandalas with leaves and flowers

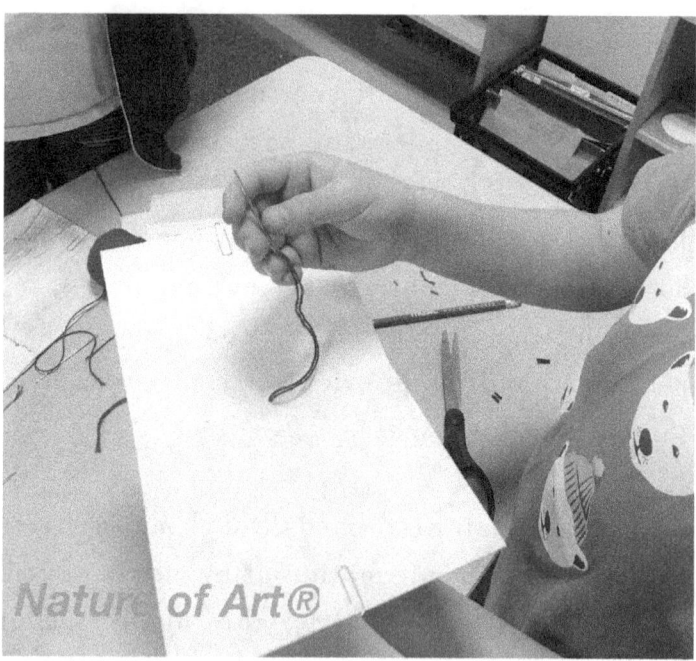
Bookbinding through stitching.

relations between elements, which develops the distinguished artist's eye.

The visual arts are a significant way to improve spatial intelligence. Visual art creation relies on spatial understanding, and art making teaches kids visualization. When children create art, they become aware of the spatial relationships between objects in the realm of their own experiences.

As they engage in two- and three-dimensional art activities, they create sight patterns stored in the mind—long-term spatial memories. Spatial construction in their mind becomes possible. This gives them the ability to visualize and manipulate elements, rotate objects, and distinguish depth and balance, which is critical in early childhood brain development and for designing with the elements and principles of design.

Children can conceptualize an idea straight from their mind, then express it in either two- or three-dimensional form, thus moving through two stages of the artistic process: imagination and construction. Visual arts are definitely one of the things that help kids understand spatial awareness around them.

Visual spatial skills are enhanced only by experience. It's important to note that spatial intelligence is something that kids cannot learn unless they are actually doing an activity; art gives them the experience of seeing how things interact and happen, dynamically or statically.

Children cannot develop spatial intelligence by viewing pictures, reading, or discussing fine art imagery alone; they must record these pattern blocks of cognitive experiences dynamically. In short, it's something we learn only by doing.

Chapter 9

Dynamic and Static Understanding

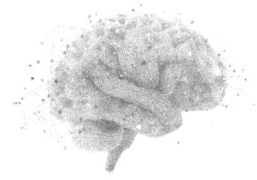

D ynamic motion is physical energy happening as a result of an action. Static imagery is the result following dynamic motion that stays at rest. It's impossible for children to truly learn visual arts without witnessing firsthand the temporal motion of sight patterns in dynamic motion.

As students develop, they can recall memories and understand more complex ideas because of their stored spatial experiences. This is why we should

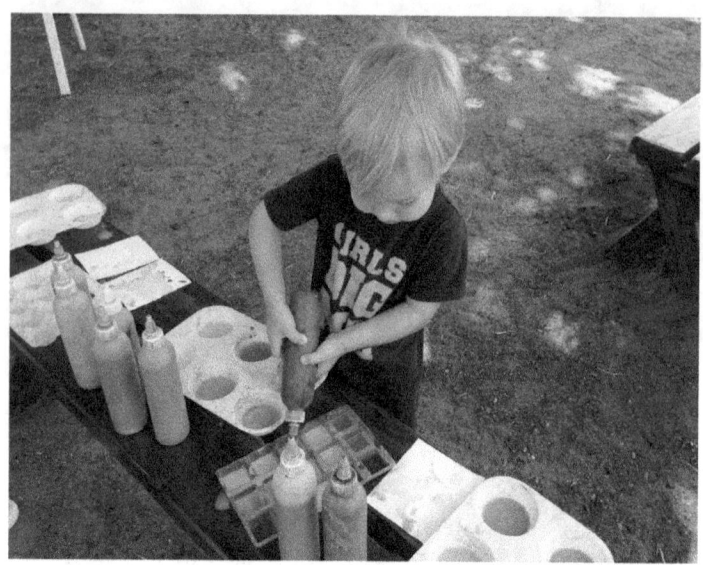

Early childhood students learning color theory with watercolor.

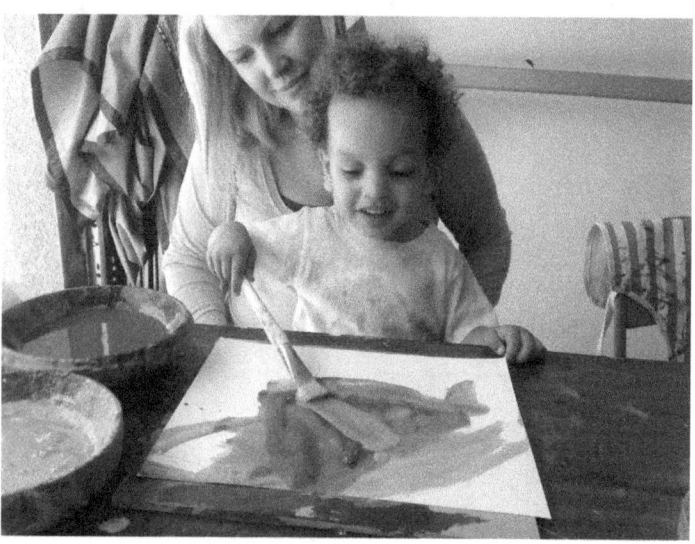

not rely on teaching children visual arts through static imagery or verbal theory lectures alone.

Studying the Masters' artwork to learn the elements and principles of design, by viewing only static imagery, is ineffective. But it is possible for children to learn later by reflecting on their own static results, following the dynamic art activities they experienced firsthand.

If you recall what I shared in Chapter 7 about visual perception, you can better understand how dynamic experiences contribute to better knowledge. Children should have ample dynamic, process-based, hands-on art experiences to develop bottom-up knowledge.

This helps them build skills in a hierarchical way, which will allow them in the future to recall top-down processed knowledge. Most young children do not have long-term memories to pull from at the beginning of their lives. They must go through the process of making art to create their own sight patterns and store them in their memory, building visual perception.

Dynamic understanding is organized knowledge

of objects in relation to oneself or a given space. This process can be learned by recalling dynamic experiences stored in memory.

Here's an example of how dynamic understanding can build artistic knowledge: As children mature and approach other art domains like learning three-dimensional drawing skills, they will be able to recall dynamic knowledge.

This understanding can recall volume concepts mapped in their memory, for example, by their experience building clay modeling forms in 3D. The students work with forms and remember the architecture of how they were constructed and that they felt like in volume.

This experience can help them create a 2D drawing that looks more three-dimensional. Witnessing dynamic motion firsthand can help record this information in memory.

In my teaching experience, adolescents and adults who lacked dynamic spatial awareness struggled to move forward in creating three-dimensional illustrations or computer graphics on a 2D plane.

They lacked dynamic energy experiences. This, of course, is an advanced idea, but young children witnessing the dynamic actions of paint splattering on paper can develop some knowledge of how paint behaves.

Watching the dynamic motion of two colors splattering and combining is very important. It is important for teaching children how to mix primary colors into secondary colors.

Allowing students to experience this firsthand is far better than showing them static imagery of two primary colors and verbally explaining how when they combine, they create a secondary color. Without witnessing it in dynamic motion, children will still lack the understanding of how it occurs.

.

Chapter 10

Getting Started With SAM, And Final Thoughts

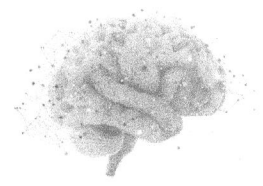

Given what you have read so far, you can see how our sensory system is connected to how we see and the actions of making art. We cannot ignore sensory neurobiology when thinking about how children learn.

Although we still have much to discover and learn about how the eyes and brain process visual information, I have shared many experiences in this book on how this method has worked in my favor for teaching children art literacy. I've created systems, frameworks, and processes for over thirty years, yielding much success.

Art Framework

In the previous chapters, I've discussed the sensory areas that make up the three key neurological components of SAM. I explained why I moved past the old model of teaching visual arts using the Old Masters' concepts to a more modern approach by considering how the child's visual system is wired.

I only discussed my theory of how children process art information; I did not explain how to teach art. You can find these ideas in my other art books. This book's framework is designed to explain how the child neurologically collects sensory information while engaged in making art.

Consider the Phases of Art Development

I witnessed children progressing through sensory experiences at different ages, which helped me create a classification of the three key phases of art development. These phases are average growth periods where I recognized that children are capable of performing certain art skills or tasks. I have classified them as follows:

- Phase 1: Young Exploratory Arts (13 months–6 years)
- Phase 2: Mid-Exploratory Arts (7–12 years)
- Phase 3: Foundational Fine Arts (12–17 years).

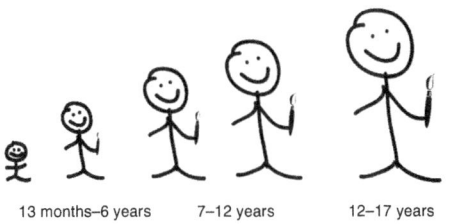

13 months–6 years   7–12 years   12–17 years

Different growth phases of art development: digital doodle from early childhood through adolescence

My longitudinal observations helped me identify a child's developmental state across all three key phases. I was able to recognize the type of teaching methods and art projects that were best suited for their developing sensory system.

These phases are not based solely on age, grade level, or academic level, but mainly on the child's exposure to art mediums, state of visual perception, fine motor movement development, cognition, and implicit memory. These ages are not precise but serve as a general marker for a normally developing child.

<u>Young Exploratory Art</u> children are seeing and experiencing art for the very first time. They don't understand the role of visual arts in their young lives. Children in this beginning phase are in a very curious state and use their mouths as sensory

detectors to explore objects. They cannot look at projects and plan with intention.

This phase is a great primer for visual art introduction and should be filled with positive tactile sensory experiences. Process-based exploratory activities are best. These children lack the visual perception and the many hours of cognitive processing and fine motor skills needed to make art.

<u>Mid-Exploratory Art</u> children can focus for up to an hour and plan art projects with simple steps. Their gross motor movements are now more refined, and they can work with basic art tools.

They have an understanding of line, shape, colors, and some composition concepts. These children can now learn basic art elements and practice in different domains of visual arts.

Children in this phase are not yet ready to focus on perspective-rendering 3D ideas. They can work with their imagination and follow along with simple guided copy-mode lessons in lines.

<u>Foundational Fine Arts</u> children are ready to study the elements and principles of design in a traditional fine art structured format. Their

attention span is much longer. They can plan and follow directions with more complex steps.

They are mature in all three key component skill sets. Their visual perception is developed to study 3D perspective illustration and painting. They can use their imagination, plan, construct, and reflect on their artworks.

For Educators

It is important that I share my findings with the teachers, researchers, and educational specialists who create art programming. I feel today's educational models are asking children to create art without teaching them foundational skill sets or taking into consideration how children learn through their senses.

It's taken me all these years to clarify those ideas and create an art curriculum that supports the sensory systems. I hope my ideas serve as a framework for schools and colleges preparing to teach early childhood and elementary grade students.

I hope I have made the case for schools to stop teaching the old, stagnant model of how the Masters learned art and adopt my new modern

Science Art Method, considering the phases of art development that children go through. There is, of course, much more we can learn and gather from modern neuroscience.

Learning Difficulties

I did not spend time discussing how this method works with children who have learning challenges. However, in all my work using this model, I've been able to adapt and modify art activities by understanding how the brain functions with the three sensory systems.

I know that visual perception is key. I've had a lot of success altering this method to suit children with challenges by adapting my teaching model while following the nature of how children develop.

There is essential research on topics like dyslexia, autism, sensory disorders, emotional trauma, or tactile and auditory sensitivities that you can turn to. I want to note, however, there's more we need to learn and discover about how children engage with art activities under these conditions. I have had opportunities to work with these children, but I have not found longitudinal studies specifically on these topics.

I do know that making art supports our senses, emotions, communication, and well-being. I implore you to try out art activities with children with learning disabilities. You might need to explore some teaching approaches such as TAB (Teaching for Artistic Behavior) methods, choice-based, or process-based art.

What's Next

As you work to make more art activities available to your students, it's my sincere hope that my Science Art Method can help you approach teaching art to children. I have spent many years creating art curriculums with this method in mind.

I developed five areas of teaching visual arts: curriculums for two-dimensional painting, drawing, color theory, and three-dimensional clay modeling and crafting. These lay the foundation for developing the three key neurological components using the SAM method. You can find many of these resources in the bibliography.

Perhaps you can take two ideas with you:
Neurons that fire together wire together, and children need more time to make neural connections.

Bibliography

Barry, S. R. (2009) Fixing My Gaze: A Scientist's *Journey into Seeing in Three Dimensions*

Barry, S.R. (2021) *Coming to Our Senses: A Boy Who Learned to See, a Girl Who Learned to Hear, and How We All Discover the World*

Cole, R.V. (1976) *Perspective for Artists*

Csikszentmihalyi, M. (1990) *Flow: The Psychology of Optimal Experience*

D'Amelio, J. (1992) *Perspective Drawing Handbook*

Eckardt, V. (1993) *What Is Cognitive Science?*

Encyclopedia Britannica, (2003) Volume 16, Colour

Gibson, E.J. (1966) *The Senses Considered as Perceptual Systems*

Gombrich, E.H. (1950) *The Story of Art*

Gopnik, A., Meltzoff, A.N., & Kuhl, P.K. (1999) *The Scientist in the Crib: Minds, Brains, and How Children Learn*

Gregory, R. (1997) *Eye and Brain*

Hoffman, D. (1998) *Visual Intelligence: How We Create What We See*

Kandel, E.R. (2016) Reductionism in Art and Brain *Science: Bridging the Two Cultures*

Karanika, M. (1997) *Visual Perception: A Cognitive Process*

Kay, L. (2020) *Therapeutic Approaches in Art Education*

Kurzweil, R. (2013) *How to Create a Mind: The Secret of Human Thought Revealed*

Lefrancois, G. (1986) *Of Child*

Macropaedia Britannica (2003) *Colour and Light*

Mann, L. & Sabatino, A. (1985) Foundations of Cognitive Process in Remedial and Special Education

Masland, R. (2020) *We Know It When We See It: What the Neurobiology of Vison Tells Us About How We Think*

Palmer, S. (1999) *Vison Science: Protons to Phenomenology*

Piek, J.P., Dawson L., Smith L.D., & Gasson, N. (2008) The Role of Early Fine and Gross Motor Development on Later Motor and Cognitive Ability

Rubenstein, J., Rakic, J., Chen, B., Kwan, K.Y., Zeng, H., & Tager-Flusberg, H. (2020) *Neural Circuit and Cognitive Development, Second Edition*

Scientific American (1974) Image, Object and Illusion

Solo, R. (1994) *Cognition and Visual Arts*

Solo, R. (2003) *The Psychology of Art and the Evolution of the Conscious Brain*

Thomas & Taylor (2003) Drawing Foundation Course

Wigan, M. (2021) *Thinking Visually for Illustrators, Second Edition*

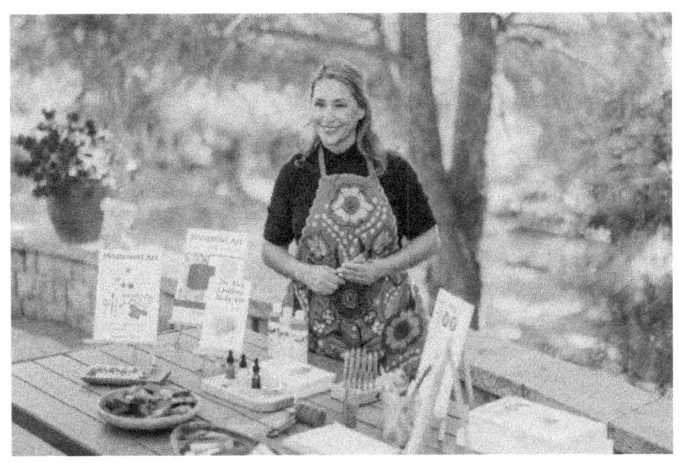

About the Author

Spramani Elaun is the author of several art education books. She is a homeschooling mom, an art teacher with a natural teaching method, and the founder of Nature of Art ® art school and art supply company. She lives in San Diego with her family.

After spending thousands of hours teaching young children art, she now supports teachers and parents on how to use her time-tested visual art methods.

Spramani teaches art classes, trains teachers, hosts art workshops at education conferences, guest speaks, and hosts art events internationally.

Her educational background includes degrees and certification in visual communication, graphic design, fine arts, painting, multimedia, offset printing, digital, and business marketing management.

Author's Contact

Spramani Elaun
Nature of Art®
P.O. Box 443 Solana Beach,
CA 92075
U.S. 1 + (760) 652-5194

http://montessori-art.com/
http://www.ecokidsart.com/

Email: Info@Spramani.com
WhatsApp: +1 (760) 652-5194
WeChat ID: Spramani-Art Teacher

Instragram
https://www.instagram.com/nature.of.art.for.kids/
Linkedin
https://www.linkedin.com/in/ecokidsart/

Hire Spramani

Spramani Elaun provides a diverse array of services aimed at inspiring and empowering individuals and organizations in art education. As a celebrated author and keynote speaker, she shares her expertise and passion for cultivating creativity. Her live workshops and teacher training programs, offered both online and in-person, deliver practical strategies and hands-on guidance for educators.

Spramani also collaborates with venues and corporations to create dynamic events that ignite collaboration and innovation. For those seeking flexible learning opportunities, her video art training and Art Teaching Blueprint™ online certification offer expert instruction tailored to your pace.

She further supports creative endeavors with premium art supply materials, ensuring quality in every project. From educational seminars to corporate events, Spramani's services are thoughtfully designed to elevate art education and inspire meaningful creativity.

Books

Nurturing Children in the Visual Arts Naturally
ISBN-13: 978-0991626403
Clay Play ISBN-13: 978-0991626441
Kids Painting ISBN-13: 978-0991626410
Kids Color Theory ISBN-13: 978-0991626434
Defining Visual Arts ISBN 978-0-9916264-5-8
Introducing Visual Arts to the Montessori Classroom
ISBN-13: 978-0991626427
Early Childhood Art Guide ISBN 9780991626496
Montessori Early Childhood Art Guide
ISBN 9780991-626472
Montessori Art: The Essential Elementary Guide - Second Plane
6-12, ISBN 9798991256100

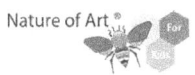

Nature of Art ®

Free Resources, follow QR codes for book enhancements

Join Spramani's Weekly Art Newsletter

Elementary Art Materials List

Phases of Art Video Training

Elements of Art List (Artsy Terms) List

Curriculums

Painting Curriculum, 57 brushstroke Lessons
Painting Work – Art Album (Montessori Elementary)
Kids Color Theory Curriculum, 37 mixing Lessons
Clay Modeling, 27 Lessons
KidsDrawing Curriculum 41 Lessons (Elementary)
Kids Drawing Curriculum 14 Lessons (Early Childhood)

Kids Crafting & Constructing Curriculum

Order Curriculum Here:

Montessori-Art.com

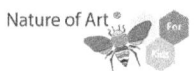

Nature of Art ®

Shop Nature of Art®
Premium Children's Art Supplies

Store.EcoKidsArt.com

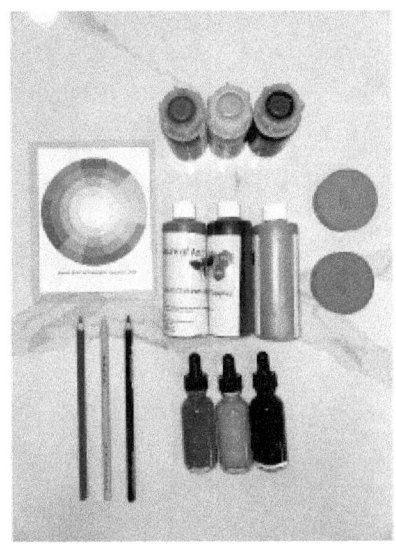

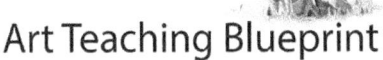

Art Teaching Blueprint

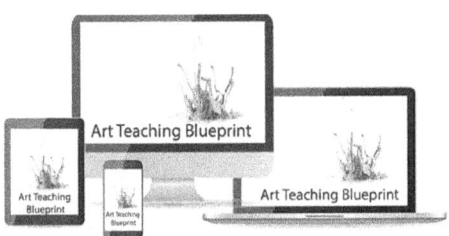

Get Art Certifed

Online Digital Course

Art Teaching Blueprint is comprehensive and broad in scope; it lays the foundation for understanding how children learn art so that you can start implementing art lessons into your classroom. Certification or self-pace is offered.

Learn more by visiting Montessori-Art.com

Book Club Discussion Questions for

The Way Children Make Art

These questions are designed to spark rich discussion and reflection, whether participants are teachers, parents, or simply enthusiasts of art and education.

1. What personal or cultural influences do you think led Spramani to teach visual arts in a way that challenges traditional norms?

2. Do you think visual arts should have a larger role in education? Why or why not?

3. How do sensory experiences, as explained in the book, contribute to the effectiveness of the science art method?

4. Can you identify any parallels between the science art method and your own teaching practices (in or outside of the classroom)?

5. What does "creativity" mean to you? After reading the book, do you believe creativity is a skill that can be taught and learned?

6. How has this book shifted your perspective on the relationship between cognitive science and art in education?

7. What does the science art method teach us about child development, and how can this help educators tailor better learning experiences?

8. Spramani introduces the concept of implicit memory in the book. How do you interpret this idea, and what role do you see it playing in how children learn art?

9. What flaws or limitations in today's art education system are highlighted in the book? What do you think can be done to address these issues?

10. After reading this book, what practical strategies can you implement to encourage both creativity and understanding of cognitive science in children's art-making?

11. What part of the science art philosophy resonated most with you, and how do you see yourself applying these principles, either as a teacher, parent, or learner?

12. Did anything in the book surprise or challenge your existing views about how children engage with art?

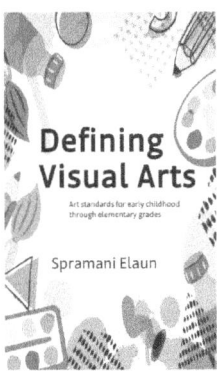

Defining Visual Arts

Get the next book in this series, Defining Visual Arts. Available in paperback and ebook. Find at most online book stores and Amazon

Visual Art Primer

A primer to understand what visual arts is, and how you're suppose to teach it. If you are in charge of teaching your visual art program this book is for you. Need to design meaningful art lessons, this book will guide you well. Understand what art curriculum should include. This book discusses up-today international art standards.

Excellent quick read, 32 pages

Defining Visual Arts is perfect for early childhood – elementary grade teachers and parents. This book provides art literacy structure.

In this book, you'll learn:

- What art literacy means
- How to meet art standards
- How artist language relates to teaching children
- What type of art projects to teach
- What art mediums are best for children
- Understand artist technique teaching
- How spatial understanding relates to the visual arts
- Understand the artist process

Notes

_____
_____
_____
_____
_____
_____
_____
_____
_____
_____
_____
_____
_____
_____
_____
_____
_____
_____
_____
_____
_____

Notes

Notes

_____
_____
_____
_____
_____
_____
_____
_____
_____
_____
_____
_____
_____
_____
_____
_____
_____
_____
_____

Notes

_____

_____

_____

_____

_____

_____

_____

_____

_____

_____

_____

_____

_____

_____

_____

_____

_____

_____

_____

_____